your DNA guide the workbook

Printed in the United States of America

ISBN 978-1-7346139-3-3 Print

ISBN 978-1-7346139-4-0 eBook

Back cover photo: Noy Lovanh
Design: Blue Kayak Productions

Your DNA Guide
724.484.3344
www.yourDNAguide.com

Hey there.
Before you dive into this DNA thing,
I just wanted to let you know that
you've got this.
You can learn this stuff.
Your ancestors need you,
so they will help,
but you probably already know
more than you think you do.

Oh, and by the way, this is a companion workbook to Your DNA Guide - the Book. The two are kinda inseparable. So if you find yourself without a copy of Your DNA Guide - the Book, head over to www.yourDNAguide.com to fix that mistake immediately.

online resources

In addition to this fancy workbook we have created an extra resource page to hold all the links we reference in this workbook. You can find all those resources at https://www.yourdnaguide.com/workbook-resources.

working your plan

Look for this icon to point you towards corresponding resources in the Book.

Look out for vocabulary words and definitions when you see a question mark.

notes

my DNA logins

This is a place to gather all the login information you have scattered around on your computer, in different notebooks, or random scraps of paper by your desk.

Consider including your logins from all five major genetic genealogy testing companies including 23andMe, AncestryDNA, FamilyTreeDNA, MyHeritage DNA, and Living DNA. If you don't have test results from all of the companies, consider our DNA testing plan on page 11 for more information. Make sure your passwords are unique to each site.

My DNA Kit

Company Name	Username or Kit ID	Password
23andMe		
AncestryDNA		
FamilyTreeDNA		
Living DNA		
MyHeritage DNA		

DNA Kit for ____________________

Company Name	Username or Kit ID	Password
23andMe		
AncestryDNA		
FamilyTreeDNA		
Living DNA		
MyHeritage DNA		

DNA Kit for ____________

Company Name	Username or Kit ID	Password
23andMe		
AncestryDNA		
FamilyTreeDNA		
Living DNA		
MyHeritage DNA		

DNA Kit for ____________________

Company Name	Username or Kit ID	Password
23andMe		
AncestryDNA		
FamilyTreeDNA		
Living DNA		
MyHeritage DNA		

my research goal

While wandering around your DNA test results might be a fun exercise for a lazy afternoon, it is not likely to produce much in the way of earth-shattering discoveries if you don't have a plan. Walk through this quick exercise to solidify your research goal (it's ok, you can change your mind later) and get this show on the road!

Now, I know you may have more than one ancestor keeping you up at night. But for the sake of simplicity and sanity, I am going to teach you how to find just one—the easiest one—to get started. Once you have mastered the steps in the DNA research process, you can come back and do this all over again with the more difficult-to-research ancestors.

Let's begin by filling out this form.

The person I want to find is the

◯ **father** ◯ **mother**

of my

◯ **parent** ◯ **grandparent**

◯ **great grandparent** ◯ **2x great grandparent**

◯ **3x great grandparent** ◯ **4x great grandparent**

Whose name was

____

who was born in

(year and place)

____

Targeted testing

Ask a relative (known or proposed) to take a DNA test to help you evaluate genetic relationships.

Now that you have the name of an ancestor you want to research, let's try to measure the likelihood of success in using DNA to learn more about this person. Basically if you can say "yes" to any of the statements below about the ancestor you just outlined, you may want to choose a different initial research goal. I know, I know, THIS is the ancestor you are desperate to document. And I promise you will get a chance to, but trust me, you want to learn on easier ones first if you can. You know, crawl before you walk, and all that.

- ◯ **I checked the 3X or 4X great grandparent box**
- ◯ **The ancestor I named was born outside the United States**
- ◯ **The ancestor I am looking for was likely born outside the United States**
- ◯ **The ancestor I named was an only child**
- ◯ **The ancestor I named only had one child**

Now, far be it from me to get between you and your discovery. Just know that as we move forward, if you said "yes" to any of the above statements, you have your work cut out for you, and you will need a fair amount of patience and a lot of persistence, and a bit of luck wouldn't hurt.

However, if it was the 3X or 4X great grandparent box you checked above, I must be up front with you: don't do it. While DNA technology is ah-mazing and can make connections between people and families that nothing else can, it does have its limitations. So if it is a more distant ancestor you seek, you need to turn to YDNA or mtDNA testing to help you. For more information on just how to do that (sorry, this workbook is all about autosomal DNA) check out the respective pages on our online Resource Page.

Autosomal DNA (atDNA)

The DNA you received from both of your parents, packaged in 22 chromosomes. (The 23rd pair are technically not atDNA, but are called the sex chromosomes).

notes

Most Recent Common Ancestor (MRCA)

Most Recent Common Ancestor (MRCA): refers to the closest ancestor—usually an ancestral couple—that connects you to a match.

my DNA testing plan

Now, we don't want to get ahead of ourselves. You can't reach your family history goals if you don't have the DNA resources you need. So before we get too far into this, let's make sure you have your DNA in all the places it needs to be to set you up for success. To be clear: depending on your research goal you may just need one single solitary DNA match to bust your case wide open. But more often than not, you will want your DNA to be looking for those Best DNA Matches in every possible nook and cranny. So let's go through the following exercise together to make sure you have set yourself up for success.

1. Is the ancestor you are looking for a male?

No? Move onto the next question.

Yes? OK, you will want to look into YDNA testing for this line. Check out our YDNA resources on the Online Resource Page. Then move on to question 2.

2. Thinking about your research goal, are there any individuals on that line in your parent or grandparent generation who have been or *could* be tested?

No? Move onto the next question.

Yes? List all the possible relatives here, as well as their relationship to your goal. For example, I might list my uncle Bob as Bob-Merla-Lucy-EKERT+PARKS-goal. In this example, EKERT+PARKS is our MRCA—the couple that Bob and I share in common. The second column helps remind you of your research goal.

Path to MRCA ancestral couple	Goal
Bob-Merla-Lucy-EKERT+PARKS	mother of EKERT

3. Still keeping your research goal in mind, are there any individuals on your generation, or the ones below you, who do not have an older generation to test, who have tested or who might test to help you in this research? So for example, Bob's mother Merla had several siblings who have grandchildren whose parents have passed. So he might want to ask them to test.

No? No relatives? You are a lone wolf? That's ok, we can still work with you.

Yes? Perfect, fill out the following table.

Path to MRCA ancestral couple	Goal
Cousin Joan-Leta-Lucy-EKERT+PARKS	mother of EKERT

Ideally you would want to go all the way back to Lucy and find descendants of her siblings to test. But hey, we know that research is rarely ideal, so we will work with whatever you have.

4. If any of the relatives you have identified in steps 2 or 3 have not tested, you will want to test them at the company that currently has the largest database and will set you up for the best overall testing plan.

We suggest testing any new people first at AncestryDNA, then transferring to MyHeritage (and paying the $29 unlock fee), and to FamilyTreeDNA (depending on your research goal, you may or may not need to pay the unlock fee) and Living DNA.

As you complete this testing and transferring process for yourself and those you have tested, check off your progress on the next page. And be sure to check the Online Resource Page for more information on Transferring, including a link to the how-to's. The Online Resource Page also includes tips on how to provide just the right information and inspiration to ask a relative to test in our Testing Relatives resource.

Tester Name	23	AN	FT	LD	MH	YDNA

Tester Name	23	AN	FT	LD	MH	YDNA

Tester Name	23	AN	FT	LD	MH	YDNA

Occasionally mtDNA will be useful in your research, but those situations are relatively few and far between, and outside the scope of this workbook. Just make sure to check out that mtDNA section of our Online Resource Page if you want to learn more about whether mtDNA testing will help you.

A quick overview of what we have just done is on pages 4 to 10 of the Book. We have only just begun with the analysis part.

Pages 11–12

5. Your test is in and you attached your DNA results to your family tree – right?

Yes? Way to go! Keep moving!

No? Hold up whippersnapper - this is a quick but needed step before you move on. Check out the Resources Page for all the how-to's if you get stuck.

Ethnicity Results

Pages 13–16

Your first stop, no matter your research goal, is your ethnicity results. Remember, these are estimates, and will be different at each company because of the different reference populations and fancy math they use. But looking at your results across different companies can help you identify trends that may ultimately lead you to a much-needed clue in your research, so let's get started.

To make the most of your ethnicity results you will want to first consider what you already know from research and family lore about your family's geographic origins. Use the modified family tree below to write down what you know about the country of birth of your ancestors. You can find a digital version of this chart in the Online Resource Page, if you want to get all fancy (and you don't mind excel or google sheets).

your dad's parents | and their parents | and grandparents

other places worth mentioning on this side of the family:

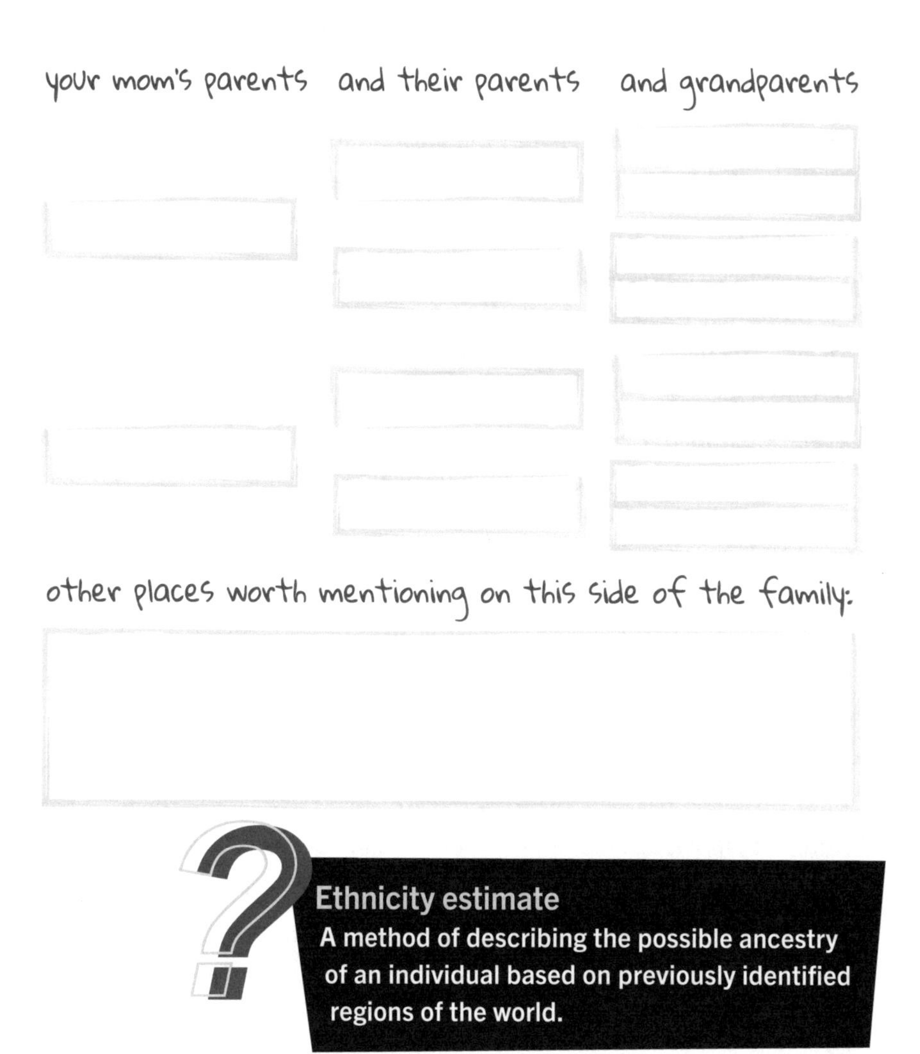

Ethnicity estimate
A method of describing the possible ancestry of an individual based on previously identified regions of the world.

For even more on how to track your own expected ethnicity, check out our Online Resource Page.

Each DNA testing company has broken up the world into a different number of pieces. To make matters even more confusing, the same general swath of land sometimes has different names at different companies. So the first step is to try to gather that information together in one place by grouping like places together.

To do that, you need to think in terms of regions and countries. To give you fair warning, this could get messy. Things will not always line up. Just try to be consistent in whatever decisions you make across the multiple testing companies. You can pay the most attention to the top percentage at the largest regional level. See the Resource Page for some examples.

To get started:

1. Log in to your first testing company and review your results. Then check the box for the region just above the chart on the next page that represents the majority of your locations. Testers with multiple dominant regions can use more than one table.

2. For each of the boxes in the table on the far left, determine which regional category is included in your results. Label it with one of these directional terms: Northern, Southern, Central, Eastern, or Western or something else that makes sense to you. Sometimes you will have percentages that roughly correspond to these broad categories, and sometimes you won't.

3. Fill in the next level of categories with those places that seem to fit that region until all of the locations in your results are represented.

4. Log into the next company and repeat this process. Try not to add a new category unless it is absolutely necessary, but instead look for how the two categories might overlap, even if they are named a bit differently.

5. Just stick to your system. Whatever you choose to do with categories at one company, just do the same at the next. For example, if at Company A you have 11% German and 3% French, but at company B they report French+German as one category and give you 20% you have basically two options:

A. You can keep the two separate categories and guesstimate the breakdown at Company B.

B. The more accurate would be to combine the two categories from Company A into 14% and add that to a new French+German category, deleting the other two categories.

Note: there are multiple tables here for you to use as you wish. You may need more than one if you have results from more than one major region. Or you may want to use one to redo your estimates after company updates. But it is important that you are recording the information for ALL of your DNA testing companies in ONE table. Consolidation is the point here.

Test taker's name ______________________

Date ______________________

Choose the region this table represents:

◯ Africa ◯ Americas ◯ Asia ◯ Europe ◯ Oceania

Location	23	AN	FT	LD	MH

Total percentage from this region:

Test taker's name ______________________

Date ______________________

Choose the region this table represents:

◯ Africa ◯ Americas ◯ Asia ◯ Europe ◯ Oceania

Location	23	AN	FT	LD	MH

Total percentage from this region:

Test taker's name ____________________

Date ____________________

Choose the region this table represents:

◯ **Africa** ◯ **Americas** ◯ **Asia** ◯ **Europe** ◯ **Oceania**

Location	23	AN	FT	LD	MH

Total percentage from this region:

Test taker's name ______________________

Date ______________________

Choose the region this table represents:

◯ **Africa** ◯ **Americas** ◯ **Asia** ◯ **Europe** ◯ **Oceania**

Location	23	AN	FT	LD	MH

Total percentage from this region:

So...? What did you learn?

Which regions are consistent across all testing companies and also found in your family tree?

Which regions seem to be outliers and therefore aren't likely to indicate a recent missing ancestor from that place?

Ok, so you know what has been verified by your results and you have recognized what you shouldn't be looking for, but what should you be looking for? Are there any locations showing up consistently across your results that are not yet present in your family tree? If so, write them down here. They could be a clue to your missing ancestor(s).

Updates To Ethnicity

Every so often our testing companies add enough new information to their databases that they want to give you an update of your results, and of course, you will want to record them. So we have created a way you can capture that information digitally so you can continually add to it. See the Resources section if you are interested.

OK, that pretty much wraps up all the pre-work you need to do before you jump directly into The Plan, and start tracking down that missing ancestor.

The rest of the workbook will function as your Research Log. As you work your way through various parts of The Plan this is where you will keep track of all of your progress and leave notes for yourself about where/how to continue each time you need to set down your research to do something much less fun like eat or sleep, or (heaven forbid) WORK!

Now, due to the very custom nature of the Book, it is a bit tricky for us to make a Research Log that will perfectly mirror your own personal path. So instead of trying to mirror your exact path, this workbook will help you capture the essential elements of your journey to help keep all the information and discoveries in one place. Remember genealogy is not always linear. It is a little bit like peeling an onion, but those tears are for joy (ok, maybe some time for frustration too).

Best Known Match (BKM)
Someone who is a descendant of the ancestor you want to research. In autosomal DNA, this will be a match who descends through a different child than your own line.

Known Matches

 Pages 44–46

my research goal

In genealogy we always start with who we know. Write down your Best Known Matches and their accompanying information as defined in the Book. Remember that your Best Known Matches are those you already confirmed how you are related, and who are also descendants from the ancestor you want to research. And don't worry, you probably won't be able to fill out the entire table on the next page right now. That's ok, we will come back to it. Here is an example to keep in mind as you move forward.

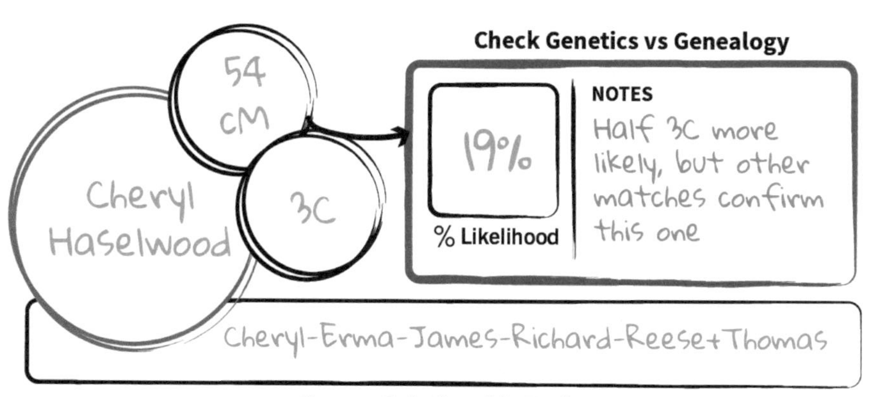

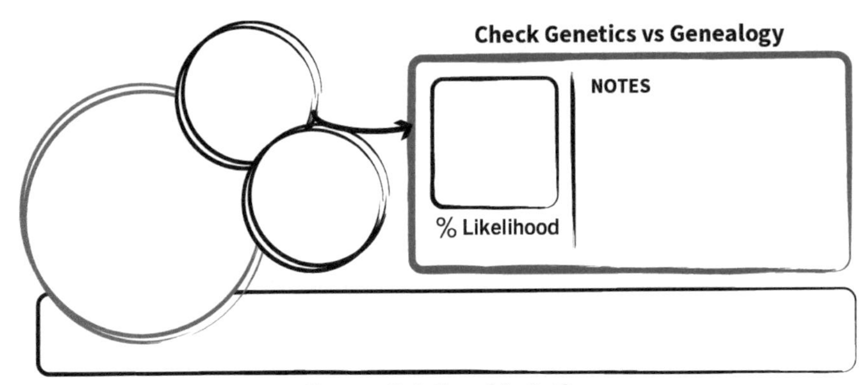
Check Genetics vs Genealogy
NOTES
% Likelihood
Known Relationship Path

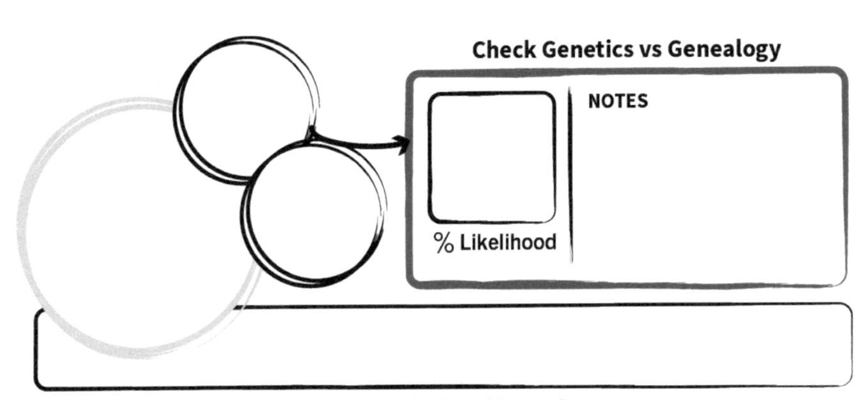
Check Genetics vs Genealogy
NOTES
% Likelihood
Known Relationship Path

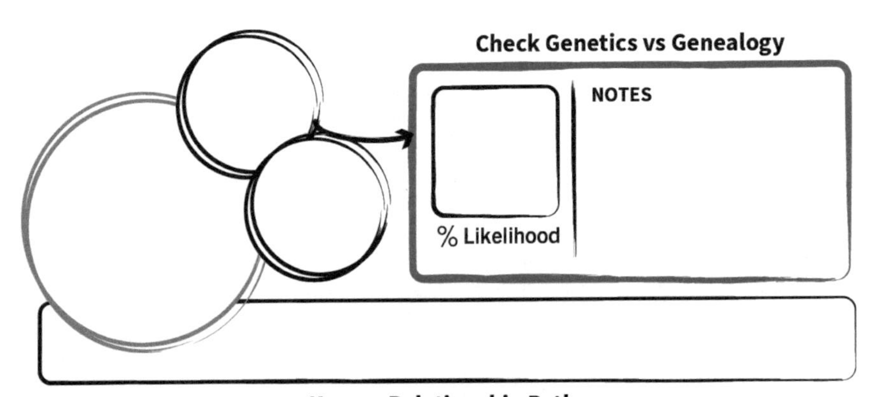
Check Genetics vs Genealogy
NOTES
% Likelihood
Known Relationship Path

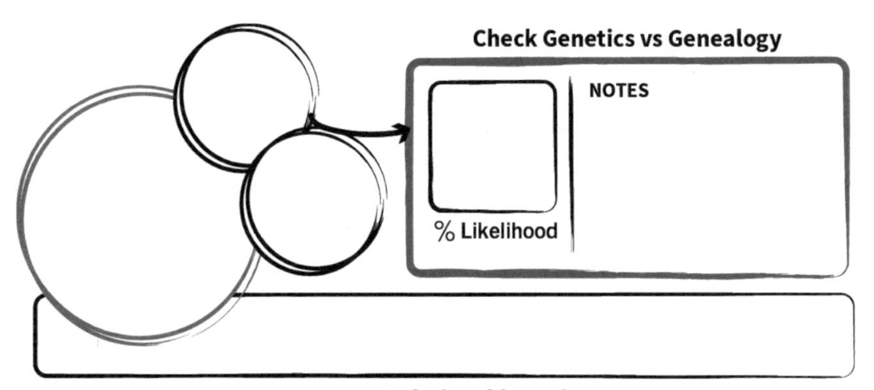
Check Genetics vs Genealogy
NOTES
% Likelihood
Known Relationship Path

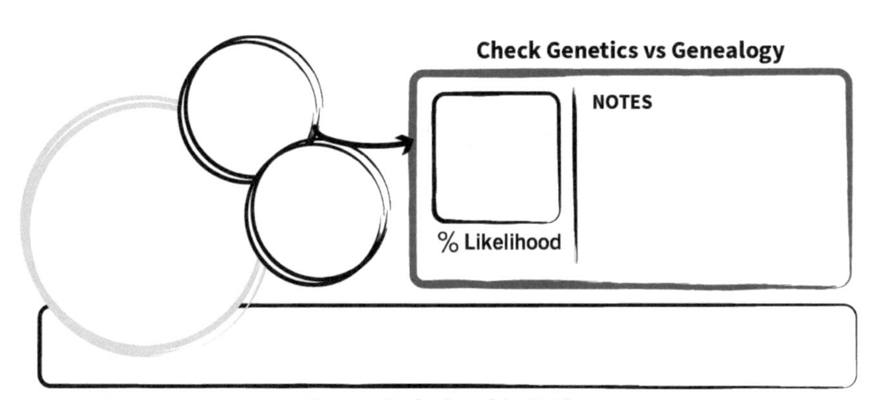
Check Genetics vs Genealogy
NOTES
% Likelihood
Known Relationship Path

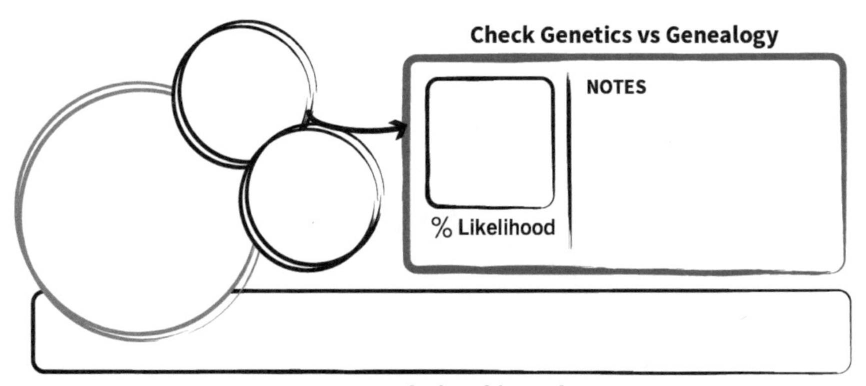
Check Genetics vs Genealogy
NOTES
% Likelihood
Known Relationship Path

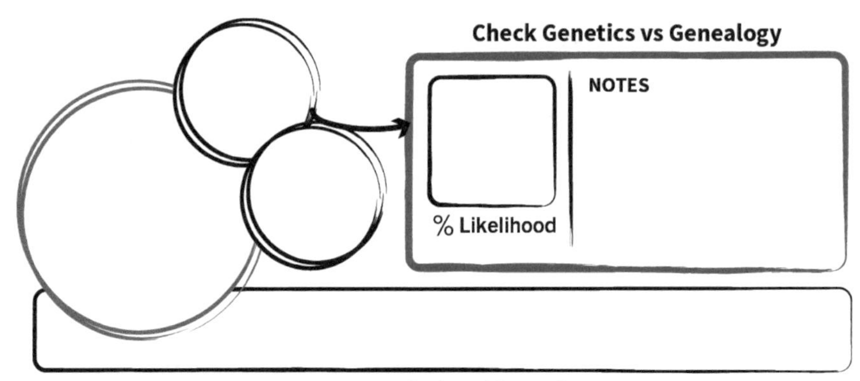
Check Genetics vs Genealogy
NOTES
% Likelihood
Known Relationship Path

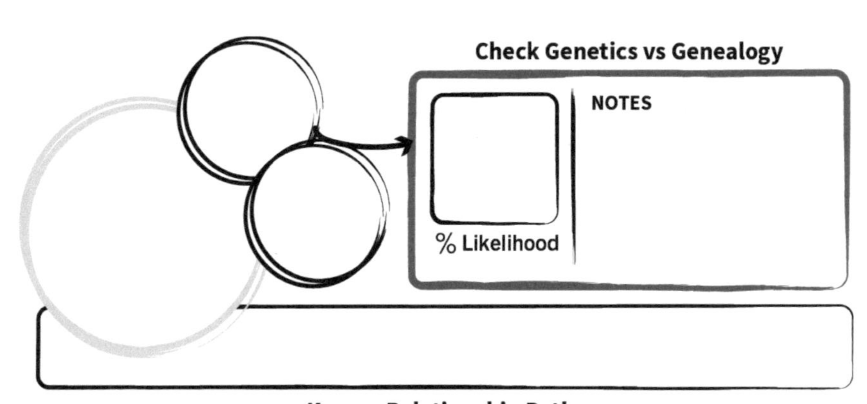
Check Genetics vs Genealogy
NOTES
% Likelihood
Known Relationship Path

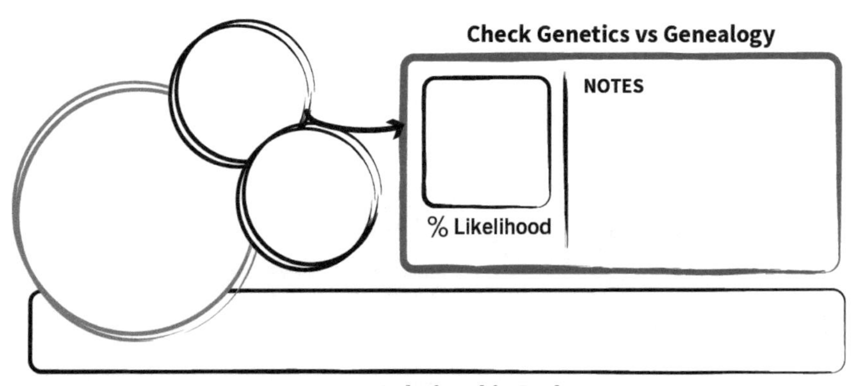
Check Genetics vs Genealogy
NOTES
% Likelihood
Known Relationship Path

Checking Genetics vs Genealogy

Page 47

Remember, these Best Known Matches are the backbone of your research, so you better be sure they are who they say they are. Otherwise your entire investigation will be down a rabbit hole in no time! You need to determine if the relationship you believe you have with your match (your genealogical relationship) is consistent with the amount of DNA you share (the genetic relationship).

There are two ways you can do this:

A If you are at AncestryDNA or MyHeritage DNA, you can use their automatic tools to help you. Just click on the relationship they provide for your cousin and review the table. Usually as long as the relationship you know you have is on the table (the higher the better), then you can consider your genealogy relationship genetically verified. If the relationship is a bit further down the chart, you may want to try another match, if you have one, just to be sure. If the known relationship is not on the chart at all, you will for sure want to use a different match.

centiMorgan (cM)

The actual definition is complicated, but you can think of it as a unit of measure reflecting the amount of DNA you share with someone (in general, the more you share the more closely you are related).

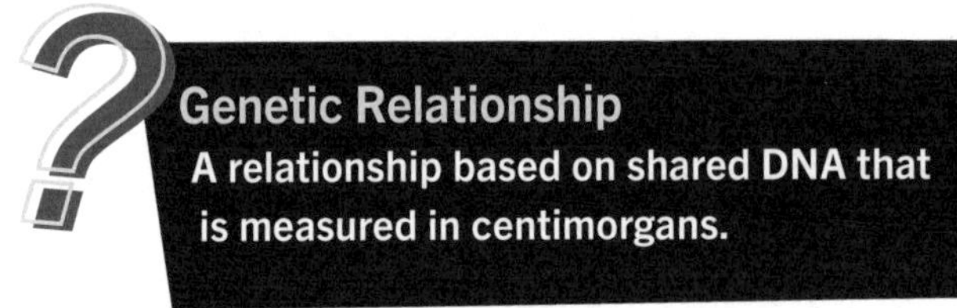

B Use the table below to look up your known relationship and the expected amount of shared DNA. These numbers come from the Shared centiMorgan Project. If you want to review the full table, you can check out our Online Resource Page. In the table, the Best Fit Range was unscientifically eyeballed based on available data and represents the range I feel like you can be REALLY confident in this genetic vs genealogy relationship, even if other numbers are actually acceptable. Essentially, it is my opinion. Take it for what you will.

Relationship	Average shared cMs	Best Fit Range
1C	866	700–1100
1C1R	433	400–600
2C	229	150–350
2C1R	122	50–225
3C	75	25–150
3C1R	48	20–100
3C2R	36	20–60

Make sure you record your check "genetics vs genealogy" findings for all of your known matches on page 28.

Best Mystery Match (BMM)
Your closest match in your target network for whom you don't know your relationship (and who has a tree).

Creating a Group with Best Known Matches

Pages 24, 44–46

OK, time to put those Best Known Matches to good use. Their number one job is to find you some Best Mystery Matches. We do this using the Shared Matches tool, and a match labeling system. Both AncestryDNA and MyHeritage DNA have in-house match labeling systems. You can read all about them (and see videos) by using the link on our Online Resource Page. If you are working in a different testing company, you will want to use the Leeds method—so visit the Resource Page for that link as well.

If you are following The Plan in the Book, I am going to teach you to make a group that is specific to the line you are researching. On Page 28 you wrote down your Best Known Matches for the line you want to research. In the box below I want you to list the ancestral couple that you share with these Best Known Matches (one of the members of this couple should be the ancestor you want to research). If you don't know both of their names, or if your BKMs are only your half cousins, that's ok, just list the one ancestor.

man who had a child with woman

Half Relationship

A relationship when you share only one common ancestor and not an ancestral couple. Example - If you and a person have the same grandmother, but different grandfathers, you are HALF first cousins. When working with DNA, this also means that any half relatives share approximately half of the expected shared cM amount.

OK, now take the two surnames of these two ancestors and write them below. So if my ancestors were Bruce Bradford who married Bertha Burns, I would write: Bradford+Burns below.

↑ This is the name of this ancestral group.

Use the list of verified Best Known Matches from page 28 to identify a Best Known Match from the above couple and write the names of at least one of them here.

Now use the Shared Matches tool on the BKM(s) above and record which color dot you used to label the matches. (Not sure what I am talking about with these dots? Make sure you review the Online Resource Page about DNA Match Labeling).

What is the Shared Matches Tool?

The Shared Matches tool is available at every DNA testing company. It acts like a filter on your DNA match list, pulling out individuals who share DNA with each other. Ideally, it helps you create groups of individuals who all descend from the same common ancestral couple.

Every time you use this procedure to create a group of DNA matches you should ask yourself: **Who did I just gather?** The answer is always the same. In the words of Dana Leeds, you will always gather His, Hers, and Theirs. Let's go back to our Bradford+Burns example. When I use the Shared Matches tool on another descendant of Bradford+Burns I will gather three kinds of DNA matches:

His: Other descendants of Bradford's parents and grandparents

Hers: Other descendants of Burns' parents and grandparents

Theirs: Other descendants of Bradford+Burns

Make sense? Good. Time to write it down. Given the network you just created, who did you gather?

his

hers

theirs

I know you just had so much fun making that network! Once you find the current missing ancestor, you will start looking for another and will need an entirely new set of networks. So here are some more of those templates so you can keep track of other networks you will make for this research goal or other research goals in the future.

man who had a child with woman

↑ This is the name of this ancestral group.

BKM

BKM

BKM

BKM

color

This is who I gathered

His

Hers

Theirs

man who had a child with woman

↑ This is the name of this ancestral group.

BKM

BKM

BKM

BKM

color

This is who I gathered

His

Hers

Theirs

man who had a child with woman

↑ This is the name of this ancestral group.

BKM

BKM

BKM

BKM

color

This is who I gathered

His

Hers

Theirs

man who had a child with woman

↑ This is the name of this ancestral group.

BKM

BKM

BKM

BKM

color

This is who I gathered

His

Hers

Theirs

As you are working The Plan you may find that in addition to the networks that are specifically aimed at finding the people you are looking for, you will find it helpful to have the other known lines in your family tree labeled. This can help ensure there aren't any multiple relationships or endogamy going on in your family tree that might throw off your group-making.

To that end, you should consider stopping and making groups to represent all four of your great grandparent couples (or as many as you know). The process is the same. Name the group with the last names of those two great grandparents.

Use the family tree below to identify your four great grandparent couples. Use the space next to their names to write out the name of that group you will create by using the last names of each person, as well as the colored dot you will use to identify them.

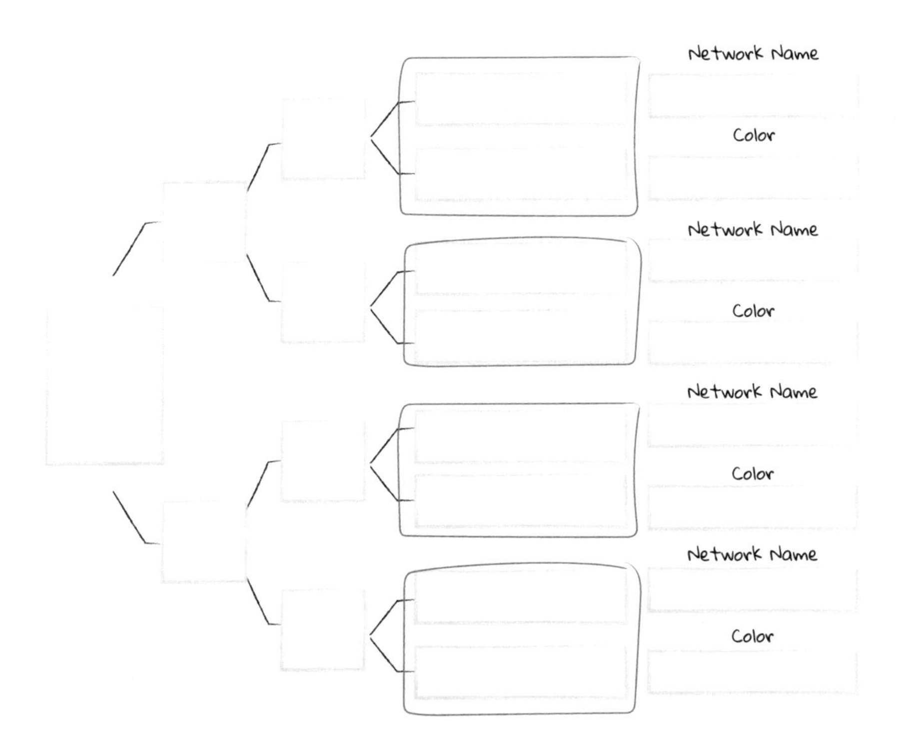

Splitting Your Network

 **Pages 222–223**

Okey dokey, now you have yourself one shiny new network that has something to do with the ancestor you are looking for. The problem is this network contains too many matches. That's right, your network with its His, Hers and Theirs is just too big. You need to try to get rid of some of those matches to give yourself the Leftovers you need. Work through this section to help you document all that fancy splitting you are learning to do in the Book.

Start with the name of your initial network. Then fill in either of the couples in the next generation. Now *I know,* you likely don't know both of these couples. That's the whole point of your search! For example I might say that Bradford+Burns is my initial couple, and Bart Bradford and Selina Dunn is in the top box and Harry Burns and ?? is in the bottom box. That shows that I am looking for the mother of my Burns ancestor.

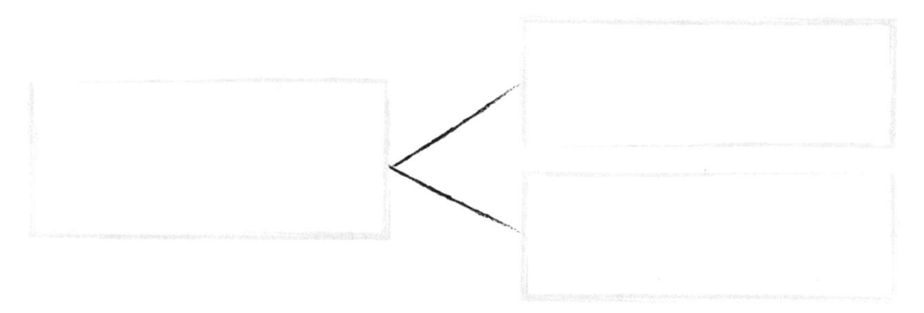

OK, whichever couple you DO know, they are the subject of your next network. So let's get going and create it! To continue my example, I would write Bart Bradford and Selina Dunn in these boxes.

man who had a child with woman

OK, now take the two surnames of these two ancestors and write them below. So if my ancestors were Bart Bradford who married Selina Dunn, I would write Brandford+Dunn below.

↑ This is the name of this ancestral group.

Who are the Best Known Matches you used to create this network? Need a refresher on who these people are? Check back on page 28 of this workbook.

BKM

BKM

BKM

BKM

BKM

BKM

Now use the Shared Matches tool on the BKM(s) above and record which color dot you used to label the matches. (Not sure what I am talking about with these dots? Make sure you review the Resource Page about DNA Match Labeling).

color

When did you last check for BMMs for this network?

date

Congratulations! You have now split your network and you should have a list of leftovers. You can identify them by reading the pattern of your dots.

1. Start by filtering your match list by the original network you created. So in our example, this would be the Bradford+Burns couple.

2. Scroll down the list until you see a match in the list who does not share the dot of the second network. In our example this is Bradford+Dunn. These matches who are Bradford+Burns and NOT Bradford+Dunn are your leftovers.

Note below the dot pattern you expect to see for your leftovers.

Initial network name and dot color

Split network name and dot color

Resulting dot pattern expected for my leftovers

You will take these Leftovers, who are your Best Mystery Matches, into the next step in your plan.

Leftovers

The group of matches that remains when you have labeled all the known matches. This group contains your Best Mystery Matches.

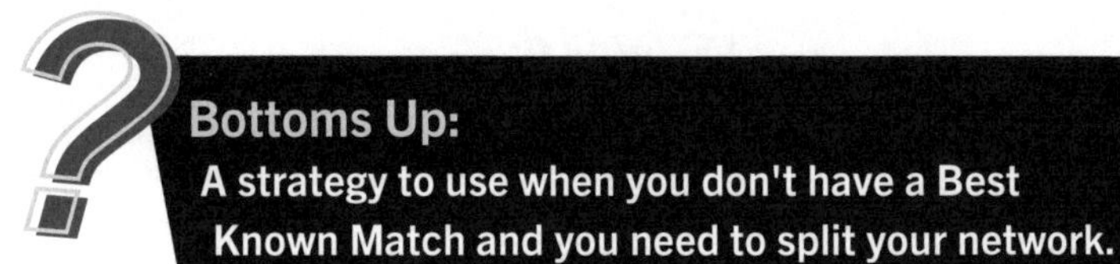

Bottoms Up

 Page 215

OK, so no BKMs to split your network? No problem. Record your Bottoms Up steps here.

Name of the network I am splitting:

Initial match I used to make Focus Group 1:

Expanded (responsibly, of course!) Focus Group 1 with the following match(es):

Initial match I used to make Focus Group 2:

Expanded (responsibly, of course!) Focus Group 2 with the following match(es):

Initial match I used to make Focus Group 3:

Expanded (responsibly, of course!) Focus Group 3 with the following match(es):

Initial match I used to make Focus Group 4:

Expanded (responsibly, of course!) Focus Group 4 with the following match(es):

Mystery Matches

Pages 18–20 & 23–24 & 40–43

Ok, you've got yourself a Leftovers network. Now for the mystery. Remember that your Best Mystery Match(es) are those who:

1. **Are in your target network (your Leftovers)**
2. **You don't know who they are**
3. **They share the most DNA**
4. **They have a posted family tree**

On page 50 you will see a worksheet to track your BMMs. Go ahead, fill out the first three boxes of the worksheet for a handful of BMMs in your target network.

Since this list might get bigger and outgrow this workbook space, you may want to make it electronically in a spreadsheet or Google sheet. If you do, take just a minute to write down the name of the document and which folder you put it in. You can thank me later.

This is where to find my Best Mystery Match list on my computer:

OK, now time to find your Generation of Connection for these BMMs in two easy steps!

Step 1: Check Birthdays

Using any information you can find (name, parents or grandparents birth years, profile picture), estimate the birth year of your DNA Match. Then compare that to the birth year of your DNA tester and decide if you think they are the same age (what I call *even*) or if the DNA match is significantly older or younger. If not *even* then you can estimate that the match is *removed*. If they seem to be just one generation removed (about 25 years-ish) then you can enter 1R for once removed in the Removed? column in your BMM tracking table. If you think it could be more like two generations different, write 2R for twice removed.

Step 2: Your Generation of Connection

Using the steps in the Book, and the resource on page 147 of the Book, write down the kind of ancestor or ancestral couple you likely share with this BMM in the table.

New matches are popping up all the time, so you will want to check for new BMMs periodically by repeating the steps you followed to create the network initially (you know, using the Shared Matches tool on your BKMs).

Generation of Connection (GOC)

The generation where you and your match share a common ancestor. Relationship estimates based on shared cM can be used to determine a likely generation of connection.

Removed

Anyone who is not on the same generation as the person tested.

Web searches for a specific ancestor's name (especially an uncommon name 3–5 generations back) may lead to individuals' posted genealogies.

Ancestry.com
(www.ancestry.com)
Search > Public Member Trees. Free users can search other users' public trees, but many things in search results are redacted unless you subscribe. Subscription options are at the country or global level; either will give you access to Public Member Tree data.

FamilySearch
(www.familysearch.org)
Search > Family Tree. Free to all users. The world's largest global, public unified family tree—see more details in the Book. Another resource is Search > Genealogies, a collection of user-submitted trees (these can't be edited or changed).

FindMyPast
(www.findmypast.com)
Search > Tree Search. This resource is strongest for families with roots in England, Scotland, Ireland and Wales, with some trees for places colonized by the British Empire. Anyone can search users' public trees, but a free user login is required to view detailed search results.

Geni
(www.geni.com)
You don't even need to log in to search this free World Family Tree ("the big tree"). In the Search People box, enter a name. Explore individual search results and click within them to see that person's tree. Advanced use options require a Geni Pro subscription; this company is owned by MyHeritage.

MyHeritage
(www.myheritage.com)
Research > Family Trees. A rich, globally-diverse resource for family trees in 42 languages. Free users can run searches, but many things in search results are redacted unless you have a PremiumPlus or Complete Plan.

WikiTree
(www.wikitree.com)
Find > Search. This free collaborative tree is smaller than the FamilySearch collaborative tree but prides itself on greater accuracy. It's searchable with your free login.

Reference for checklists on the next few pages

Best Mystery Match Worksheet

for my mystery match ______________________

This match is in the network called:

Using the chart below, cross off all the relationships that are not at the level you believe your relationship to be. So if you think your match is 1R, cross off all the relationships that are not removed.

Based on your predicted relationship, what is your generation of connection with this match? Meaning how far back in this match's tree will you need to go before you are likely to find your common ancestor? Use the resource on page 147 of the Book for help.

Kind of ancestor you likely share:

1C ☐	2C ☐	3C ☐	4C ☐	Other ☐
1C1R ☐	2C1R ☐	3C1R ☐	4C1R ☐	
1C2R ☐	2C2R ☐	3C2R ☐	4C2R ☐	

No Tree? Record the ways you have tried to identify this match. See page 141 in the Book for inspiration.

Now it's time to: **DO GENEALOGY** for this mystery match:

Research Log

I contacted this match on

I took the following actions to try to build a quick and simple tree for this DNA match:

(For help building these quick and simple trees see page 164 in the Book and read "How to Search Public Family Trees" on the Resource Page for even more tips and screenshots.)

I searched: (see reference checklist on page 49)

- [ ] Ancestry.com
- [ ] FamilySearch
- [ ] FindMyPast
- [ ] Geni
- [ ] MyHeritage
- [ ] WikiTree

What I found:

Best Mystery Match Worksheet

for my mystery match ______________________

This match is in the network called:

Using the chart below, cross off all the relationships that are not at the level you believe your relationship to be. So if you think your match is 1R, cross off all the relationships that are not removed.

Based on your predicted relationship, what is your generation of connection with this match? Meaning how far back in this match's tree will you need to go before you are likely to find your common ancestor? Use the resource on page 147 of the Book for help.

Kind of ancestor you likely share:

1C ☐	2C ☐	3C ☐	4C ☐	Other ☐
1C1R ☐	2C1R ☐	3C1R ☐	4C1R ☐	
1C2R ☐	2C2R ☐	3C2R ☐	4C2R ☐	

No Tree? Record the ways you have tried to identify this match. See page 141 in the Book for inspiration.

Now it's time to: **DO GENEALOGY** for this mystery match:

Research Log

I contacted this match on

I took the following actions to try to build a quick and simple tree for this DNA match:

(For help building these quick and simple trees see page 164 in the Book and read "How to Search Public Family Trees" on the Resource Page for even more tips and screenshots.)

I searched: (see reference checklist on page 49)

- ☐ Ancestry.com
- ☐ FamilySearch
- ☐ FindMyPast
- ☐ Geni
- ☐ MyHeritage
- ☐ WikiTree

What I found:

Best Mystery Match Worksheet

for my mystery match ____________

This match is in the network called:

Using the chart below, cross off all the relationships that are not at the level you believe your relationship to be. So if you think your match is 1R, cross off all the relationships that are not removed.

Based on your predicted relationship, what is your generation of connection with this match? Meaning how far back in this match's tree will you need to go before you are likely to find your common ancestor? Use the resource on page 147 of the Book for help.

Kind of ancestor you likely share:

1C ☐	2C ☐	3C ☐	4C ☐	Other ☐
1C1R ☐	2C1R ☐	3C1R ☐	4C1R ☐	
1C2R ☐	2C2R ☐	3C2R ☐	4C2R ☐	

No Tree? Record the ways you have tried to identify this match. See page 141 in the Book for inspiration.

Now it's time to: **DO GENEALOGY** for this mystery match:

Research Log

I contacted this match on

I took the following actions to try to build a quick and simple tree for this DNA match:

(For help building these quick and simple trees see page 164 in the Book and read "How to Search Public Family Trees" on the Resource Page for even more tips and screenshots.)

I searched: (see reference checklist on page 49)

- ☐ Ancestry.com
- ☐ FamilySearch
- ☐ FindMyPast
- ☐ Geni
- ☐ MyHeritage
- ☐ WikiTree

What I found:

Best Mystery Match Worksheet

for my mystery match ______________________

This match is in the network called:

Using the chart below, cross off all the relationships that are not at the level you believe your relationship to be. So if you think your match is 1R, cross off all the relationships that are not removed.

Based on your predicted relationship, what is your generation of connection with this match? Meaning how far back in this match's tree will you need to go before you are likely to find your common ancestor? Use the resource on page 147 of the Book for help.

Kind of ancestor you likely share:

1C ☐	2C ☐	3C ☐	4C ☐	Other ☐
1C1R ☐	2C1R ☐	3C1R ☐	4C1R ☐	
1C2R ☐	2C2R ☐	3C2R ☐	4C2R ☐	

No Tree? Record the ways you have tried to identify this match. See page 141 in the Book for inspiration.

Now it's time to: **DO GENEALOGY** for this mystery match:

Research Log

I contacted this match on

I took the following actions to try to build a quick and simple tree for this DNA match:

(For help building these quick and simple trees see page 164 in the Book and read "How to Search Public Family Trees" on the Resource Page for even more tips and screenshots.)

I searched: (see reference checklist on page 49)

- [ ] Ancestry.com
- [ ] FamilySearch
- [ ] FindMyPast
- [ ] Geni
- [ ] MyHeritage
- [ ] WikiTree

What I found:

Best Mystery Match Worksheet

for my mystery match ______________________

This match is in the network called:

Using the chart below, cross off all the relationships that are not at the level you believe your relationship to be. So if you think your match is 1R, cross off all the relationships that are not removed.

Based on your predicted relationship, what is your generation of connection with this match? Meaning how far back in this match's tree will you need to go before you are likely to find your common ancestor? Use the resource on page 147 of the Book for help.

Kind of ancestor you likely share:

1C ☐	2C ☐	3C ☐	4C ☐	Other ☐
1C1R ☐	2C1R ☐	3C1R ☐	4C1R ☐	
1C2R ☐	2C2R ☐	3C2R ☐	4C2R ☐	

No Tree? Record the ways you have tried to identify this match. See page 141 in the Book for inspiration.

Now it's time to: **DO GENEALOGY** for this mystery match:

Research Log

I contacted this match on

I took the following actions to try to build a quick and simple tree for this DNA match:

(For help building these quick and simple trees see page 164 in the Book and read "How to Search Public Family Trees" on the Resource Page for even more tips and screenshots.)

I searched: (see reference checklist on page 49)

- ☐ Ancestry.com
- ☐ FamilySearch
- ☐ FindMyPast
- ☐ Geni
- ☐ MyHeritage
- ☐ WikiTree

What I found:

Best Mystery Match Worksheet

for my mystery match ____________________

This match is in the network called:

Using the chart below, cross off all the relationships that are not at the level you believe your relationship to be. So if you think your match is 1R, cross off all the relationships that are not removed.

Based on your predicted relationship, what is your generation of connection with this match? Meaning how far back in this match's tree will you need to go before you are likely to find your common ancestor? Use the resource on page 147 of the Book for help.

Kind of ancestor you likely share:

1C ☐	2C ☐	3C ☐	4C ☐	Other ☐
1C1R ☐	2C1R ☐	3C1R ☐	4C1R ☐	
1C2R ☐	2C2R ☐	3C2R ☐	4C2R ☐	

No Tree? Record the ways you have tried to identify this match. See page 141 in the Book for inspiration.

Now it's time to: **DO GENEALOGY** for this mystery match:

Research Log

I contacted this match on

I took the following actions to try to build a quick and simple tree for this DNA match:

(For help building these quick and simple trees see page 164 in the Book and read "How to Search Public Family Trees" on the Resource Page for even more tips and screenshots.)

I searched: (see reference checklist on page 49)

- [ ] Ancestry.com
- [ ] FamilySearch
- [ ] FindMyPast
- [ ] Geni
- [ ] MyHeritage
- [ ] WikiTree

What I found:

Best Mystery Match Worksheet

for my mystery match ______________________

This match is in the network called:

Using the chart below, cross off all the relationships that are not at the level you believe your relationship to be. So if you think your match is 1R, cross off all the relationships that are not removed.

Based on your predicted relationship, what is your generation of connection with this match? Meaning how far back in this match's tree will you need to go before you are likely to find your common ancestor? Use the resource on page 147 of the Book for help.

Kind of ancestor you likely share:

1C ☐	**2C** ☐	**3C** ☐	**4C** ☐	**Other** ☐
1C1R ☐	**2C1R** ☐	**3C1R** ☐	**4C1R** ☐	
1C2R ☐	**2C2R** ☐	**3C2R** ☐	**4C2R** ☐	

No Tree? Record the ways you have tried to identify this match. See page 141 in the Book for inspiration.

Now it's time to: **DO GENEALOGY** for this mystery match:

Research Log

I contacted this match on

I took the following actions to try to build a quick and simple tree for this DNA match:

(For help building these quick and simple trees see page 164 in the Book and read "How to Search Public Family Trees" on the Resource Page for even more tips and screenshots.)

I searched: (see reference checklist on page 49)

- [ ] Ancestry.com
- [ ] FamilySearch
- [ ] FindMyPast
- [ ] Geni
- [ ] MyHeritage
- [ ] WikiTree

What I found:

Best Mystery Match Worksheet

for my mystery match ______________________

This match is in the network called:

Using the chart below, cross off all the relationships that are not at the level you believe your relationship to be. So if you think your match is 1R, cross off all the relationships that are not removed.

Based on your predicted relationship, what is your generation of connection with this match? Meaning how far back in this match's tree will you need to go before you are likely to find your common ancestor? Use the resource on page 147 of the Book for help.

Kind of ancestor you likely share:

1C ☐	2C ☐	3C ☐	4C ☐	Other ☐
1C1R ☐	2C1R ☐	3C1R ☐	4C1R ☐	
1C2R ☐	2C2R ☐	3C2R ☐	4C2R ☐	

No Tree? Record the ways you have tried to identify this match. See page 141 in the Book for inspiration.

Now it's time to: **DO GENEALOGY** for this mystery match:

Research Log

I contacted this match on

I took the following actions to try to build a quick and simple tree for this DNA match:

(For help building these quick and simple trees see page 164 in the Book and read "How to Search Public Family Trees" on the Resource Page for even more tips and screenshots.)

I searched: (see reference checklist on page 49)

- ☐ Ancestry.com
- ☐ FamilySearch
- ☐ FindMyPast
- ☐ Geni
- ☐ MyHeritage
- ☐ WikiTree

What I found:

Now it's time to bring these Best Mystery Matches together and draw them into a tree. There is space here on this page if you want to sketch it out, but we recommend you use a large sheet of paper or use Lucidchart. See the Resource Page for more information.

Doing Genealogy

Pages 25–26

OK, if you haven't yet done so, take just a moment to celebrate how far you have come! Seriously. Great job. Let's recap your achievements to this point:

1. **You created a DNA Network.**
2. **You identified a Best Mystery Match, and likely Best Mystery Matches.**
3. **You probably spent some (or a lot of!) time DOING GENEALOGY to build out the trees for these Best Mystery Matches.**
4. **You have identified a common ancestor, or ancestral couple for these Best Mystery Matches and drawn them out in a tree.**

Phew! That's a lot of work.

Now comes the fun part!

It's time to DO GENEALOGY to figure out how YOU are connected to the tree you have created for your shared matches. Ideally, you would read the chapter on WATO in the Book (page 168) and use WATO to help you figure out your connection. For more help with WATO, see our Resources page.

WATO, What Are The Odds?
A tool at DNA Painter that uses probabilities to hypothesize your relationship to a group of shared DNA matches who all descend from a common ancestor.

You can use the space below to record your login to DNA Painter (the website that hosts the WATO tool) and the name of the family tree you have created, as well as your observations.

My login:

My WATO tree name:

Before we dive into the analysis, let's just run through a couple of things to see if we can be as sure as we can be that you set up your WATO tree correctly. Just to make it easier to talk about, we are going to say that we are trying to figure out how YOU fit into this tree, and we set up this WATO tree according to *your* DNA matches.

- ◯ **I entered all of the cM values according to the actual amount of shared DNA I found between the match and myself.**
- ◯ **I did not enter any of my siblings or close known family members into the WATO tree.**
- ◯ **I entered ALL of the DNA matches I found connected to the tree, no matter how much DNA they were sharing (I didn't just pick those who shared the most).**
- ◯ **I added birth years whenever possible.**

If any of the above were not done, you need to go back and do them before we move on with your analysis.

WATO says that the most likely way I connect to the tree is:

(example: I am the great granddaughter of Horace Wheatly through one of his four daughters).

WATO gives the above scenario a score of

This scenario could be supported by my genealogy research because:

This scenario could be refuted by my genealogy research because (really try hard here to think of reasons why this might NOT be true!):

If your top hypothesis is 100 times more likely than the next one, you probably don't need to fill out the rest of this worksheet.

The next most likely scenario has a score of

and suggests that my relationship is:

This scenario could be supported by my genealogy research because:

This scenario could be refuted by my genealogy research because (really try hard here to think of reasons why this might NOT be true!):

Just for fun, let's list at least one more possible scenario!

The third most likely scenario has a score of

and suggests that my relationship is:

This scenario could be supported by my genealogy research because:

This scenario could be refuted by my genealogy research because (really try hard here to think of reasons why this might NOT be true!):

Additional notes or observations:

-
-
-
-
-
-
-
-

notes

Ask The Wife

 **Pages 212–214**

Remember that the Ask The Wife Strategy is useful when you have identified a common ancestor with your genetic network, but you just aren't entirely certain where you fit into that family tree. Ask The Wife is really about identifying the genealogical connections between your separate DNA networks. If you find yourself using this strategy, use the worksheet below to help you keep your research organized.

Name of the ancestral couple you have identified in common with a DNA Network:

↑ Identified Ancestral Couple

Use the handy-dandy chart on the next pages to list their children and spouses (including the spouse's surname and birthplace when you have it!) and record what you have done to "Ask The Wife!" For example, you may need to first DO GENEALOGY to actually find the spouse. Then you will want to search your match list by this spouse's surname to see if you find any matches. If you don't find any matches right away, just move onto the next spouse, knowing you may need to circle back.

If you do find matches it is time to DO GENEALOGY and build the trees of these matches to see if you can see a connection between this match and the spouse.

But I am probably telling you what you already know, since you have read the Book! So just move on to the worksheets on the next pages and get some research done!

+

Child Spouse

Checklist	Notes
◯ Searched for this surname in my match list. List the matches here. If you don't find this surname in your list, move onto the next spouse	
◯ Built family trees for these matches. Note here where that tree can be found.	
◯ Used shared matches on these matches. Note the label you gave them and the dot color. List some of them here and note if they connect to the tree.	

+

Child | Spouse

Checklist	Notes
◯ Searched for this surname in my match list. List the matches here. If you don't find this surname in your list, move onto the next spouse	
◯ Built family trees for these matches. Note here where that tree can be found.	
◯ Used shared matches on these matches. Note the label you gave them and the dot color. List some of them here and note if they connect to the tree.	

+

Child Spouse

Checklist	Notes
◯ Searched for this surname in my match list. List the matches here. If you don't find this surname in your list, move onto the next spouse	
◯ Built family trees for these matches. Note here where that tree can be found.	
◯ Used shared matches on these matches. Note the label you gave them and the dot color. List some of them here and note if they connect to the tree.	

+

Child Spouse

Checklist	Notes
◯ Searched for this surname in my match list. List the matches here. If you don't find this surname in your list, move onto the next spouse	
◯ Built family trees for these matches. Note here where that tree can be found.	
◯ Used shared matches on these matches. Note the label you gave them and the dot color. List some of them here and note if they connect to the tree.	

If you run out of spouses and you still haven't found your missing network, you may need to go forward or back a generation in this tree and start again.

If you still have trouble, you might want to take a more genetic approach and just look for the genetic network in your DNA match list that maps to this section of your tree. The Counting Cousins strategy on page 219 in the Book might help.

Next Steps

Now that you have a hypothesis about how you fit into that tree for your DNA matches, it's time to (you'll never guess) DO GENEALOGY! YES!!! Finally! Right?! Enough with all this DNA stuff!

So given the connection you think you see between your line and this new family, what are the steps you can take to verify that connection with genealogy records? It starts with writing a clear research question.

Your research question will likely look something like this:

Was

(name of your last known ancestor)

the (circle one)

child, grandchild, great grandchild,

of

(name of the common ancestor you found in WATO)

?

What is your genealogy research plan? Keep track of your progress using the pages provided at the end of this workbook.

And if you get stuck, we highly recommend the Search Party Course (www.thesearchpartymethod.com). The Search Party Course helps you gather and organize your genealogy and gives you a step-by-step plan to methodically work through genealogical resources to ensure you have not missed anything.

Of course, we here at Your DNA Guide want to continue to support you on your journey. So please be sure to visit your Resource Page for next steps with us.

But mostly, we just want you to feel like you are a little bit (or a lot!) closer to better understanding how your DNA can work with the paper research to help you tell your story.

Just 'cause I thought you might need it, below is an official diagram of Your DNA Guide - the Plan. Hopefully you will find it useful as you work your way through the Book and the Workbook.

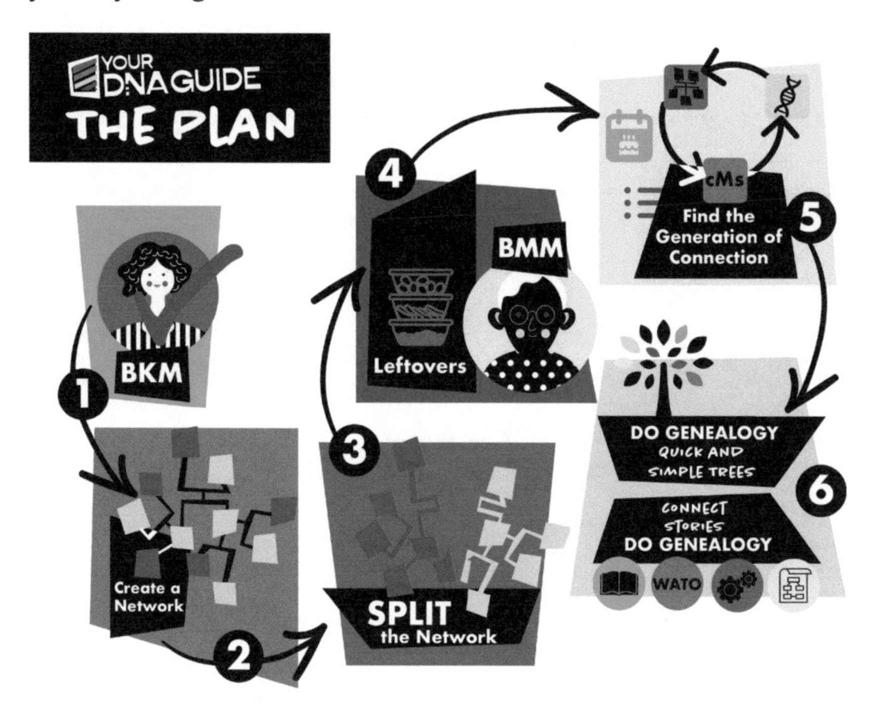

notes

notes

notes

notes

notes

Made in United States
Troutdale, OR
11/20/2024

25093125R00053